THE
THEATRE
POET

First published 2020

Published under licence by Brown Dog Books and
The Self-Publishing Partnership, 7 Green Park Station, Bath BA1 1JB

www.selfpublishingpartnership.co.uk

ISBN printed book: 978-1-83952-109-6
ISBN e-book: 978-1-83952-110-2

Cover design by Andrew Prescott
Internal design by Andrew Easton

Printed and bound by CPI Group (UK) Ltd, Croydon, CR0 4YY

This book is printed on FSC certified paper

FSC

www.fsc.org

MIX
Paper from
responsible sources
FSC® C013604

THE THEATRE POET

DAMIEN POOLE
FOREWORD BY
AMANDA HOLDEN

A COLLECTION OF
MODERN THEATRICAL POETRY

BROWN DOG BOOKS

Foreword

'I had the pleasure of meeting Damien Poole back in 2011, when we were both cast in Shrek the Musical at the Theatre Royal Drury Lane, Covent Garden. I was playing Princess Fiona, and Damien had the convivial task of lifting me each performance as intimately as a cast mate may, one bum cheek in each hand, up into the air, whilst dressed as a tap dancing rat. It was quite a show that holds so many memories for me.

One Christmas Eve during the run of Shrek, Damien sat us down and read the most wonderful poem to us all during our cast physical warm up, which was based on the famous 'Twas The Night before Christmas'. He had transformed the story into a hilarious piece of verse that included every one of us in the cast, I remember everybody crying with laughter. I'm not sure he knew back then what talent he had in writing poetry. We were all transfixed.

So when Damien sent me his draft of 'The Theatre Poet', I wasn't surprised he'd written it.

I was blown away by its magic, and I could see myself in so many of the characters he'd created, as I'm sure you all will if theatre is in your heart, as it is in mine. Stories of backstage, on stage, theatre etiquette, theatre mice, (I've met plenty of those in my dressing rooms!)

Damien is a storyteller, someone who understands people and their emotions, and how theatre catapults those emotions into the spotlight. That's where this book of Theatrical poetry is destined to be, centre stage, lapping up the standing ovation it deserves'

Amanda Holden.

A Collection of Modern Theatrical Poetry

Introduction

Writing poetry was something that found me.
I was far too busy pirouetting and sweating in fat suits in London's
West End to be serious about literature and poetry.

Yet after many years of working in theatre, I found a love for
limericks and rhyme, often writing poems for cast members who were
leaving or for opening night cards.

Theatre and poetry go hand in hand for me now,
and you're holding the result, a book of theatrical poetry, with beautiful
drawings by the talented Mary Warren.

I hope you enjoy them as much as we do.

Damien Poole

Contents

A Moment In Time 10

Theatre Etiquette 16

You Won't Get An Applause 31

The Theatre Mouse 39

Treading the Boards 45

His Memory 51

Her Memory 58

Waiting Game 66

The Theatre Mirror 76

The Bedpost Ribboned Ballet Shoes 84

The Doubting Gremlin 92

The Real Ghost of Drury Lane 98

Marjorie and I 112

The Fan 122

Bubbles and Bunty 126

What Happens When the Magic Ends? 133

Physiotherapy 138

He Loves The Sound of Music 142

Take a Picture 147

There is swearing in this collection.

Sorry Mum.

A Moment In Time

Sequins, feathers, hat and cane.

Excited crowds, October rain.

Orchestration, harp, piano.

Crowds dissolve in fading shadow.

Beating hearts and palpitations.

Silent murmurs, new sensations.

Dreams in minds of young and old

As curtains open, plots unfold.

Recalled memories, laughter, tears.

Exposed feelings, uttered fears.

Accomplished actors storytelling.

Charged, inspiring and compelling.

A family of friends, together by fate,

With a common desire to create something great.

A flurry of weeks that mean more than you know.

Gone in a flash, with so few to go.

An opening night, a company bow,

Proud to be here, the back of a cow.

A memory forever, a moment, a team.

We created together a theatrical dream.

Theatre Etiquette

The lights have dimmed, the curtain up, at last Act 1 has started.

Already someone's crunching crisps and the gent behind has farted.

The child is crying next to me and all I want to do,

Is pour my wine over his head and wet the bugger through.

I keep my cool and hope for once I may perhaps enjoy,

This play I've sold a kidney for, for just two hours of joy.

Alas, the woman next to me is jeering at the stage.

It's taking all my might not to slap her face with rage....

        Instead I take my wine glass and without a single curse,

        I pour the remnant Chardonnay into her open purse.

Latecomers are walking in, sidestepping towards me.

And of course, to no surprise he stands at six foot three.

Irritant and sweating I no longer see the stage.

But still I keep composure – and still I hold my rage.

The audience at last dissolves into a muted hush.

Time for me to finally enjoy my theatre rush.

(Silence / Muted Hush)

Flash! He's taking photos! This idiot I see.

The usher's still not looking, I guess it's down to me.

With a rage I rise, like a phoenix taking flight,

Who would take on any bugger that dare ruin theatre night.

'Turn your bloody phone off, you irritating cock!!'
And without a thought I'd done the deed and stood with stifled shock.

No patron now would dare to move, or cough or sneeze or moan.
No noisy conversations, or texting on their phone.

No more farting patrons, just an audience confusion;

'How dare this person stand mid-show and ruin the illusion!'

The usher walks t'ward me, which is blatantly unwise,

Especially the moment his torch shines into my eyes.

In front of everybody, this jumped-up little git,

Has told me to be quiet and has told me I must sit.

Shouting across the aisle I tell him, 'Don't you fret,'

'I'm the only bugger watching who's got theatre etiquette!'

I've made my point, and with retained composure I ignore,

The fact the man with IBS has now begun to snore.

But still this will not faze me, I hold my beating heart,

Praying all will end well, before Act 2 can start.

(Bliss)

FIRE ALARM!

FIRE ALARM!

The noise deafens my ear

As the light begins to rise and my eye begins to tear.

Who'd have thought some bugger could have set off such a thing,
On the night I chose to come and see the players dance and sing!?

The audience dissolves under fire exit sign.

I unveil my Chardonnay and pour a second glass of wine.

Finally there's silence, no patrons here to fight.

Finally a granted wish, my treat on Friday night.

But alas the jumped-up usher shouts;

'Are you wishing to be dead?!'

With unyielding theatre etiquette,

Chardonnay's poured on his head.

You Won't Get An Applause

Show business is tiring,

Rehearsals every minute,

Hot summer days, backstage,

Can push you to your limit.

Matinees are painful,

And shows whilst you're hungover,

Sometimes make you feel your life,

Is almost nearly over!

But could you live without it?

And work a 9 till 5?

Would it be fulfilling?

Would it make you feel alive?

There is one thing we all receive,

That fulfils all our cause.

If you work in show business,

You always get applause!

You could become a cleaner,

And dance washing the floors.

You'd smell of bleach and polish,

But you won't get an applause.

You could work as a plumber,

And twist a pipe or two.

But does a plumber get applause?

I don't think that they do!

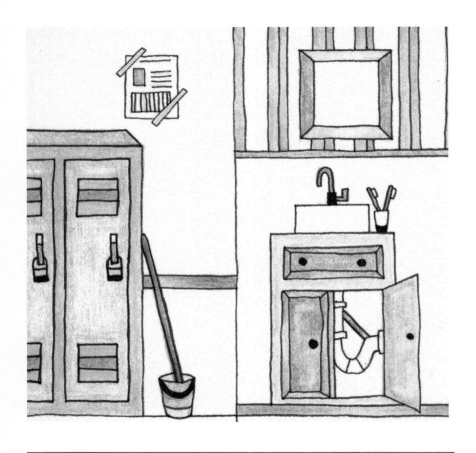

Maybe a dermatologist,

And wash those weary pores.

Skin you've always dreamed of,

But you won't get an applause.

So as you walk to theatreland,

And enter your stage doors.

Remind yourself of what you have,

And soak in that applause!

The Theatre Mouse

Why is it you scream at me when I come out to play?
Why not stop to talk to me? Instead you run away.

I am the theatre mouse, dear heart, do not feel bereft,
I was cast in pantomime and then I never left.

If only you would stop a while to listen to a mouse,
The stories that I have to share, are juicy back of house.

So please be kind and offer up a smelly bit of Cheddar,
Then sit with me and I will tell you stories for the pleasure.

Us mice are theatre oracles, the keepers of the show,
What stories would you like to hear, what would you like to know?

Perhaps the understudy who put soap upon the stair,
Or the dresser who cut off her leading lady's hair.

The two from the ensemble who were having an affair,
They did it in the dressing room, they did it everywhere!

So when you see a mouse run past don't run from me again,
I'm probably due on the stage and lost my hat and cane.

Don't attempt to poison me, I'll know it when you do,
That's the only time I leave a trail of mousy poo!

I live in every nook and cranny, in every wall and heater,
Amongst the leading actresses in every major theatre!

I dream of tapping on the stage, I will I'm sure one day,
Perhaps appear in 'Our Mouse' or a mousy Shakespeare play.

So next time I appear inside your bag or in a shoe,
Give a smile and tilt your hat and say, 'Mouse! How'd you do?'

Treading The Boards

Could you ever have foreseen that you'd be living in a dream
Of step ball changes, pirouettes, leaps and backstage etiquette.
Side stage changes, costume mends, true meaning of contract friends.
Understand the highs and lows of epic one year contract shows.

A lead,
       a swing,
              an understudy.

                                        Calling everybody 'lovey'
Jockstraps, bras and bums galore..

            Upstage,

                            downstage,

       backstage tour.

Curtain up,

Erupt applause, stand behind the waiting gauze.

A ballet, a song, a scene, a verse. Forgetting lines,

(could it be worse?)

Jazz,

Contemporary,

Tap and Street.

Arms in bras bas.
Pointed feet.
Opening nights.
Theatre awards.

A job, a dream, treading the boards.

His Memory

The Man

'My legs feel stiff most of the time,
my back is feeling sore,
I often cannot make it even to the bathroom door.
I used to be so agile,
I could leap into the air.
But now my legs don't work for me,
I can't move from this chair.

I know no one is listening,

but still I tell my tale,

If I stop I know this tattered memory will fail.

There is one nurse who holds my hand and sits as my narration,

Becomes a seated version of a stage show animation.

She smiles at all my memories, which set my young soul free,
And unbeknown to her she means an awful lot to me.

I used to be an actor.
A life upon the stage,
A flurry of ambition, an audience to gauge.

A show that filled my heart with song, this man of eighty three,
Was part of all the magic,
a Sondheim show, 'Gypsy'.

I know you won't remember, but the laughs we had ring still,
And all my heart belongs to it,
A dream it would fulfil.

It played at the Savoy, you know, the show, it went so fast,
It had the greatest score,
Oh nurse
It had the greatest cast.

I played a boy called Kansas, and the back end of the cow.
Oh nurse, how could it all fly by?
How could I allow?

I'd tread the boards in tap shoes.
I'd sing my song aloud,
My mother and my father came to watch, they were so proud.

Those days are sadly over,

My long-gone West End shows,

But still I have a sparkle in my eye that never goes.

So when I sit upon this chair, and close my eyes I see,
That audience – upon their feet,
Smiling back at me.

Don't think of me as eighty three. Instead, try to allow,
Your mind to see me proud to be…

The rear end of the cow.

Her Memory

The Nurse

He'd sit amongst the other folk and tell his story loud.

Always with a smile and more than often feeling proud.

But nobody would listen,

It was only me,

Who'd spend the time to sit with him and listen thoughtfully.

You see I'd heard this story told many times before,

The other nurses, they would say, had found him such a bore.

But this old man was special.

I'm sure he couldn't see,

That unbeknown to him he meant an awful lot to me.

In his time he'd tread the boards too many times to say.

Several years in West End shows,

A short time on Broadway.

But this story was his favourite,

This man of eighty three,

The time he'd spent at the Savoy, in a Sondheim show,

'Gypsy'.

What's special was, I'd been there.

A girl of twelve no less.

I'd told him this so many times, but his memory weren't the best.

If not for his Alzheimer's,

I'm sure that he could see,

The Gypsy show he talked about had meant the world to me.

At sixty one I'm no spring chick – but memories still flow,
Of the day we went to town to see a West End show.

I sat in true bewilderment of the magic b'fore my eyes,

The dancing cow,

The showgirls,

The bows and the reprise.

An actress full of wonderment. A theatre affair.

'I want to be on stage, Mummy!
I want to be up there!'

And I did become an actress, my dreams they all came true,
If only I could tell this man

'It's all because of you'.

Those days are sadly over,

a long-gone West End show,

But just like you I have a sparkle that will never go.
So as you sit and close your eyes, I dream that it were true,

You'll see me in the audience,

smiling back at you.

Waiting Game

He smiled at me as I'd walked in so surely that's a sign,
He said I'd hear today for sure, he will, you're right, it's fine.
It's just I hate the waiting game not knowing what will be,
Is the West End calling, or back to KFC?

The audition was a triumph and the panel were a dream,
What an opportunity to join that perfect team.
You should have heard the joke I made, they'd laughed, so that's a sign,
But had they really liked my scene? They did, you're right, it's fine.

Any minute now he'll call – my agent, he's a star,

He says that I'm a triple threat.
He says that I'll go far.

But still he hasn't called me, I've been waiting on the line,
Any minute now he'll ring, I'm sure he will. It's fine.

(Checks phone is not on airplane mode)

(Turns phone volume up to highest setting…

Waits at least three minutes)

Ok.

I know that it's a faux pas but I've just come off the phone.
I left a fleeting message on my agent's answerphone.
Asking why he hasn't called, maybe it's a sign,
Just to calm my nerves a tad, I've poured a glass of wine.

(Glug)

I messed up all my lyrics so there's no recall in sight,
I'm taking off these tap shoes now to settle for the night.

Perhaps the phone has broken?
All calls perhaps decline?

As each hour passes now I fear the job's not mine.

I'd had to hide my Dairy Milk, the girls were eating dust.
So takeaway delivery is surely now a must.

Disastrous audition, the West End's yet to shine.
Time to dance the conga on the unemployment line.

My agent is an idiot!

A useless, arsing knob!

I'm a triple threat goddammit
yet he can't get me a job?

And now I'm fat and ugly.
Maybe it is time,
To leave my bloody agent.
The stupid bloody swine.
I'm totally a failure.
This business ain't for me.
I've waited now for two whole hours,
I've lost my sanity.
I'd rather be a waitress.
It's where my stars align.
I'll never be an actress,
I'm a triple shite combined.

I love my gorgeous agent!

He's just rung with the news,
He said I've got a recall,
I've cracked open more booze.

I knew that he would call me. I told you I'd be fine.
The bright lights now are beckoning and the lit-up name is mine!

The Theatre Mirror

Today I passed a mirror and I stopped in true surprise,
The lady staring back at me I barely recognised.
A face began to wrinkle on this lady that I see.
A woman turning 60…

A decrepit OAP.

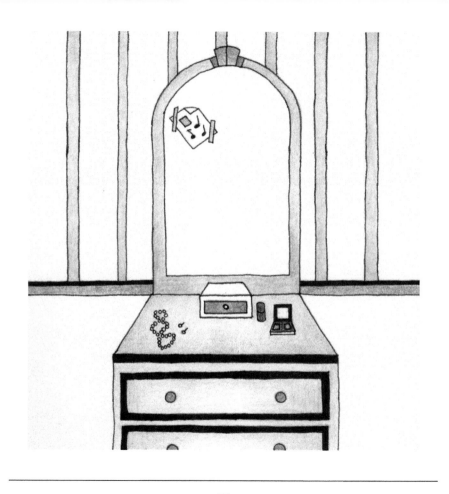

But there's something that's familiar,

A girl I recognise.

With an impish sort of sparkle that shines deep within her eyes.

I see a pirouetting shadow,

Full of hope and song.

I see a showgirl longing for the past that's sadly gone.

I see a mother standing proud of all that she's achieved.

Worth the pain and anguish and the dreams she had to cease.

The failures and successes, rehearsal and audition.
Curtain calls and costume changes.
Her feet in fifth position.

I see the cat that sat aside Dick Whittington 'neath lights.

I hear applause,

Bulb-lit stage doors

and nerves on opening nights.

Yet that girl would never frown or moan or wish her time away.
She'd point her toes and kiss the air and dance another day.

But now all I have are memories of the days of yesteryear..

Yet do I frown or worry?
Do I moan or shed a tear?

No.

I think of all that I've achieved, the life that I have led.
Just 'cause I'm a pensioner doesn't mean I'm bloody dead!

I have my constant laughter.
I still have dreams to dream.
I still have things to smile about,
I still have self-esteem.
I am my own creation.
A person standing proud.

I point my toes,

I dance my dance,

I sing my song aloud.

I sing still in the shower. I dance still in the rain.
I am amazing as I am, impossible to tame.

So as I look into my eyes, I smile with doting glee,
Knowing that the sparkle shall forever live in me.

The Bedpost Ribboned Ballet Shoes

At the time I couldn't hear the words they'd said to me.
I had no time to understand, it started suddenly.
A pain each time I took a step, an ache each pointed toe.
An hour, a week, a month went by, yet how was I to know?

A specialist appointment, next day a consultation.
The words poured through like water, 'You must have an operation.'
Soon after they were spoken, all at once I knew,
The words would fall into a void, the day they'd said it's true.

Never to dance another step, their dark, painful confession.
Never to stand on stage again, 'Dance can't be your profession.'

I took my pointe shoes out of their case and laid them on the bed.
I stood a while, deep in thought at what the doctors said.

As tears escaped, I tried to stand with both feet on the floor,
And said aloud, 'I'll prove you wrong, I'll dance again once more.'

I tied my shoes onto my bed and tried to fall asleep,
Knowing that my promise was a promise hard to keep.

The morning after, I awoke and pain dissolved my mind.
I tried to see my future but the past was all I'd find.

I turned to put my light on, and there for me to see,
Were my pointe shoes tied with ribboned pink, looking back at me.

I smiled the widest smile you've seen, a warmth swelled in my core.
With all my might I dragged my legs and feet onto the floor.

My ballet shoes stayed tied onto my bedpost day and night,
They kept me strong each day I nearly lost the endless fight.

They willed me to be stronger and to live the dream I dreamed.
They kept me strong each morning, at least that's how it seemed.

Now it's ten years later.

My feet still feel quite sore.
But I walk through Covent Garden and I walk through the stage door.

My dream, you see, came true for me,
I dance on stage each night,
There is no better feeling.
There is no stronger fight.

I make my family proud of me each night I take my bow,
I live for dance, I live for life, I live for here and now.

My bedpost ribboned ballet shoes stay with me every day,
Hung in every dressing room and there they proudly stay.

I thank them every morning for the fight through all the pain.
My bedpost ribboned ballet shoes gave me strength to dance again.

The Bedpost Ribboned Ballet Shoes
was a poem that was written for a friend of mine, Lauren.

It's a true story.

She's since been in dozens of West End shows,
Despite being told she'd never dance again.

The Doubting Gremlin

Positive	Negative

Positive

You know the words,
You know your lines.
Be confident, be strong,
This audition will go swimmingly,
You'll get the job.

                                 You're wrong.

You will I promise,
Just ignore the Gremlin in your
head,

                                 You'll mess it up.

You won't.

                                 You will,
Just head back home to bed.

Positive	Negative
	You don't know what you're doing,
	Your confidence has gone,
	You still don't know the script
	and blatantly don't know the song
You've sung the song a hundred times,	
It's always a success.	
Ignore your inner Gremlin cause.	
	It's sure to be a mess.
It really won't.	
	It will,
	You're not cut out for this career.
	There is still time to leave the room,
	You're overcome with fear!

Positive

Negative

You're far too old to play the part,

Just look around and see,

Everyone's a model,

and under twenty-three.

The part's a 'doting mother'
with a child, you silly dick!
Just go and face the panel,
you'll be fine.

Nah you'll be sick.

Sick down your blouse, forget your
words,

Then throw up on the floor.

You'll start to cry and scream

'I cannot do this anymore!'

Positive	Negative
Stop being so ridiculous!	
Your name's being called, so hurry.	
Shoulders back, be confident, it's	
time	
	Yep, time to worry.
Here we go, deep breathing.	
Show them what you've got.	
You'll get the job,	
Enjoy yourself.	
You're fine	
	Oh no you're not.

The Real Ghost of Drury Lane

The wind tore past my shoulders, as I struggled to make sight
Of the shivering tourist shoppers heading home out of the night.
T'was a stormy London eve, full of clouds depicting fear.
As the heavens poured I pulled my hat down past my bloodless ears.
The day'd grown ever bleaker and to shelter from the rain,
I crossed the cobbles of Covent Garden down to Drury Lane.
As an actor at the Theatre Royal, I'd grown numb to the tales
Of the ghosts who walked through walls and ghoulish whispering and wails.

Be it known, I relished silence, and was happy being alone.
Until the day she showed herself and made herself quite known.

It was barely early evening yet the sky'd begun to dim,
The rain soaked through my shirt and grew more heavy on my skin.

The Theatre Royal rose amongst the rooftops dipped in shadow,
And I'm doubtful I'd have stepped inside if I'd known how she would
harrow.

It was at this very moment, and still I can't explain,
I saw a figure staring at me from a window pane.

A chill rose through my spine, looked again and as I feared,

The ghostly face in shadow had completely disappeared.

The stage door sign amongst the mist appeared within my sight,
Yet the darkness had eroded any warmth I'd feel that night.
Despite my heavy heart I felt some comfort knowing soon,
I'd shortly be enveloped in my west wing dressing room.
Stage door was not a haven of home comforts one might think,
With a rotting threadbare carpet and four walls painted in pink.
The stage door keeper barely rose her head from her TV,
She grunted, sighed and slowly put into my hand a key.
I turned around in time to see the scuttles of a mouse,
Dart underneath the wooden door that led to back of house.

As I walked my heart was pounding and I tried to disengage,
Any thoughts of supernatural as I walked across the stage.

The darkness took my sight and as I stumbled past the set,
I tried to make out shapes ahead, a woman's silhouette.

My heart raced ever harder and I blinked a single tear,
As the shadow passed me slowly and it whispered in my ear.

I ran into the stairwell and the thought came once again,
That perhaps I would be happier back outside in the rain.

My room resided three floors up the cold and winding stairs,
And with a heartbeat in my ears, completely unawares.

The sound of heavy shoes were running up behind my own
And a heavy smell of lavender displaced rodent pheromone.

My hand trembled as I reached the door and fit the key inside,
And as the lights shook suddenly, the door swung open wide.

Without a hesitation, I ran through and tried to gauge,
A realistic comprehension what I'd heard crossing the stage.

The room felt cold and eerie, but I knew to my frustration,
That the ghostly things I'd seen were surely just imagination.

Taking off my sodden shirt my heart began to slow,
My hands began to warm, and my cheeks began to glow.

The ghostly goings-on took on a role of less concern,
And my mind began to concentrate on scenes I'd yet to learn.

With script in hand I sat in silence, with hope that I'd improve,
Not noticing my coffee cup slowly start to move.

A smash!

And with a fright, I jumped up out of my chair,
I looked around my dressing room,

Nobody was there.

With darted eye I saw the cup rolling on the floor,
My gaze rose and to my horror,

Something flung open the door.

I stepped towards the hallway,
Nothing could I see,

I slammed the door shut once again and locked it with the key.

There was no one else due in yet, so how could it be true,
That I felt a sudden presence and a sense of déjà vu?

There was something in the room with me, but what, I didn't know,
I had to wait and see – if this shadow now would show.

Bu when it came to nerves, I was barely now equipped,
I sat down once again and retired to my script.

Suddenly the lights turned black, yet still I turned to stare,
At a figure slowly cross the room and walk t'wards my chair.

Silence screamed around me, then with a desperate plea,
A voice echoed around the room,

'Do you remember me?'

Over again and over, the question shattered through,
I closed my eyes and without pausing shouted,

'Yes I do!'

The apparition vanished, and with nothing more to fear,
I opened up my eyes…

…and my shadow disappeared.

Marjorie and I

We'd found a deal on seats.com,

Well, Marjorie, not me.

She googled on her iPad, whilst I was making tea.

Her daughter said she swore by it

So I told her she should try,

To get some discount theatre tickets,

For Marjorie and I.

She found some for a bargain with
'audience participation'.
We weren't too sure, but at twenty quid we both felt pure elation.
So down we went to London.
A bargain on a coach.
It's not too bad (but full o' folk you'd rather not approach)

I'd made us homemade sandwiches,
Marjorie brought pie.
We drank a shandy, raised a toast to Marjorie and I.

Soho we were bound for.

We'd walked 'cause it was cheap.

Plus Marjorie needed lubricant for Mr Parson's Jeep.

Quite desperate to take our sandals off we searched for bars to try,

And found one selling 'Orgasms' did Marjorie and I.

HICK

Somehow we were running late.

(Marjorie's fault, not mine)

She'd been dancing on the table when she'd kicked the glass of wine.

Merlot down my cardigan.

Wine on pleated skirt.

The topless bar man shushed me as I screamed and went berserk!

Ten quid of coral cotton, ruined, but with no time to cry,

The show was nearly starting, we were late, Marjorie and I.

We took our seats in darkness,
Amongst the shushing hordes,

We were sweating and exhausted as the cast took to the boards.

We sat in true bewilderment.
There were no words to say.

This was no Lloyd Webber, or an opera, nor a play.

We watched with bated breath as a ping pong ball took flight,

That took refuge in my cleavage after POPPING with its might.

One after another, they appeared from deep within.

We tried but could not figure how a dozen could fit in.

It wasn't what we'd paid for,

But we asked the question why…

The OAPs were loving it!

Marjorie and I.

After this night of pure burlesque
We cried with shrieking joy.

As Marjorie admitted that she'd
'bought us each a toy.'

She opened up her handbag
and there for us to try were…

A bag of

Bouncing
Ping pong
Balls!

for Marjorie and I!

The Fan

I'm the number one fan of the leading man,
Him there, that's right, he's Peter Pan.
I've seen his Hamlet, it was divine,
He stole the play, not one fluffed line.

I'm not crazy like the stage door creeps,
I don't watch him as he sleeps.
Honestly, I'm not obsessed,
I didn't watch when he undressed.

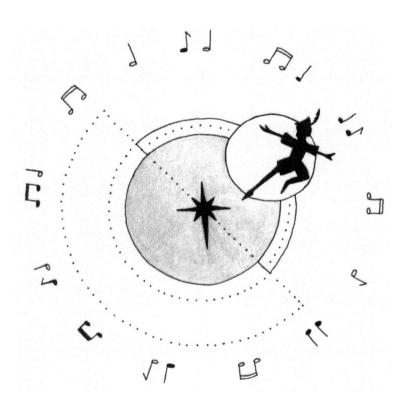

That wasn't true! Pure allegations,
Based on very loose foundations.
I got the job here months ago,
I'd no idea he was in this show.

I watch him in the stage left wing,
Perfect spot to hear him sing.
An angel's voice, I love that man,
Not love just, like, a devoted fan.

I think he winked, but the lights are dim,
His thighs look strong in those tights he's in.
One show last week, his dresser fell.
Three flights of stairs, broke like a shell!

Her skull was fractured, broken wrist,
Then guess who got asked to assist?
I'm now his dresser, maid and keeper.
The leading man's backstage Grim Reaper.

Bubbles and Bunty

Bubbles and Bunty
A troublesome two,
A duo's adventure,
If only you knew
Of the stories they shared
On their journey around,
Every new theatre,
In every new town!

You've never heard laughter I gladly would bet,
Till Bubbles and Bunty you'd finally met.

They toured as an ABBA act named 'Stout Super Troopers',
And travelled the country in an old Mini Cooper.

Through Bradford and Leeds, a stop for a wee,
Across into Cardiff and down to Torquay.

But Bunty the driver, and here I'm being kind,

Was, how should I put it?

Partially blind.

As she sped through the city, she saw blue light flickers,

Bubbles and Bunty wet both of their knickers.

Gestured to stop, they both turned to gasp,
Bunty had blatantly driven too fast!

As they pulled up their Mini, with a shivering fright,
They gasped as the policeman came into their sight.

A gorgeous young uniformed man in his prime,
Meant Bunty would surely confess to her crime!

But with manners exemplary and perfect white teeth,
A bulge in his pocket and muscles beneath.

Bubbles and Bunty knew just what to say,
'Cause these two big mamas love all of the gays!

Without hesitation they jumped out the car,
And sang out the lyrics of 'Chiquitita'!

He cheered and applauded and not before time,
took out of his pocket and ripped up the fine!

Bubbles and Bunty despite them being frugal,
Looked for a Specsavers close by on Google!

They'd both learnt their lesson and never would dare,
Leave without bringing some knickers as spare!

What Happens When the Magic Ends?

What happens when the magic ends? A loss of true romance,
Of a love that was so passionate turned into song and dance.
The dream that kept you going strong yet is all that holds you back,
The dream you can't afford to dream, so much to give, yet lack.

The pool of light that used to shine and open every door,
Is the spotlight that is dimming yet illuminates each flaw.
What would you do? Would you stay to see the curtain rise,
Or would you leave before your cue long gone before reprise?

Another twelve auditions for a job that starts next year,
Another six months out of work, another day to fear.
When you can't afford to pay the fare to travel to audition,
With a group of people half your age there is no competition.

What happens when the magic ends yet too scared to admit,
That the magic is dissolving, but afraid to now commit.
I'm 'lucky to be up there' and 'I'd do that job for free'.
With mouths to feed and bills to pay, come, take my job and see.

Of course I feel I'm lucky, and my dreams are highly sought.
But these dreams are hard to hold onto.

Much harder than I'd thought.

What happens when the magic ends?
When the tummy feeling's gone.
When the passion turns to stress then surely how I'm feeling's wrong?

A family you yearn to see can lose our loving grip,
When we have to work on Saturdays and Sundays,
Off they slip.

Every day's a memory of the things you've yet to see.
A stage that you must walk upon and what will be, will be.

So, what happens when the magic ends?
When the velvet curtain falls?
When the lights begin to dim,
When you've heard your last applause.
A new path is awaiting you, breathe in, no need to fight.
Take your final bow and smile.
You're going to be alright.

Physiotherapy

I'm waiting in the waiting room,
Aching with pure fright.
As I know that soon my physio,
Shall pummel me with might.
And I'll muffle all my screaming,
But I'll try to find a smile.
When she asks me:
'Is the pressure good?'
The answer takes a while.

But I muster,

'Yes, that's fine'

As she dislocates my spine
And I try to think of something else
To try to pass the time.
I slyly look towards the clock,
How long must this go on?
Twenty minutes still to go.
The clock, it must be wrong.

'Turn over and lean forward,
Put your arms behind your head'

No, I'd rather lie on nails
Or maybe wax my legs instead.
But I do as I am told.
My hands curl into fists,
And I'm moulded into shapes
Made only for contortionists!

He Loves The Sound of Music

My little boy is singing.
He's dancing with a broom.
He's dressed as Julie Andrews
And is spinning round the room.

He's climbing every mountain,
With a wig of tomboy hair.
He's reached the grassy hilltop,
(He's on the dining chair)

He's lined up all his teddies,
Plus the dog and ginger tabby.
Asking why on earth Maria's
Been singing in the Abbey.

He wants lessons for his birthday,
To learn to play guitar.
He plays 'Best of Julie Andrews'
On repeat when in the car.

He's asking awkward questions,
Like 'What is Do Re Mi?
What note will follow La?
What accompanies his tea?'

He hides beneath his duvet.
'I'm scared,' but still he sings,
And he's telling me he's not quite sure
what are his favourite things.

Yes, he loves The Sound of Music.
With passion through and through,
And I'll climb every mountain
Just to make his hopes come true.

He must follow his own rainbow,
And live life a scene by scene.
And I promise to endeavour
That he follows every dream.

Take a Picture

The final scene,
The last emotions,
Silent wings.
No loud commotions.
Melancholy thoughts of past.
The final show,
The very last.

A team of friends who worked as one,
Months of laughter,
Weeks of fun.

Lights dim,
The time is here,
Take my hand,
Wipe off a tear.

The final bow,

Step t'ward the stage.

Chapter ends.

The final page.

Close my eyes,

Hold the dream,

Happiest I've ever been.

No idea if I'll be back,

Empty stage, lights go to black.

Thank you for sharing this theatrical poetry journey with me.

I hope we go on many more.